Writing
Warmups

1000+ Prompts to Get Your Mind and Pen Moving

❧ Tim Haag

nfp

NO FRILLS PRESS • 2140 NW Elmwood Place • Corvallis, OR 97330-3930, U.S.A.

info@nofrillspress.com • www.nofrillspress.com

Published by No Frills Press
2140 NW Elmwood Place
Corvallis, OR 97330-3930, U.S.A.

info@nofrillspress.com
www.nofrillspress.com

Slinky® is registered with Poof-Slinky, Inc.
45400 Helm Street, Plymouth, MI 48170-0964

Library of Congress Cataloging in Publication Data
Library of Congress Control Number: 2005901305
Haag,Tim Haag
Writing Warmups: 1000+ Prompts to Get Your Mind and Pen Moving

ISBN 0-9765632-5-8
Library of Congress Control Number: 2005901305

Introduction:

You've seen it a million times— the movie director sits in a canvas chair, snaps up the megaphone, and yells, "ACTION!"

And the scene begins.

In this book, I'm the director.

Each of these prompts is a call for 'ACTION!'.

And it's up to you to write your way out of them. Or further into them. Or to ad lib a whole new scene.

Whatever gets your mind and pen moving and it really doesn't matter which moves first.

So how exactly can you parlay these ideas into an effective 'writing warmup'?

My favorite method is focused visualization.

I'll start with the prompt: *This was no time to hide.*

Recalling my days as a journalism student, I ask myself:

· *Who?* Who is hiding or at least thinking about hiding? You? Your friend? Your imaginary friend? (Yeah, I had a few as well.)

· *What?* What is happening around the character(s)? Between them? (This is a perfect spot to record some vivid sensory details.)

· *When?* When is this scene taking place? Morning? Dead of night? Ten years ago?

· *Where?* Where is this scene taking place? In a dark room? In a cave? A train station? (This too invites sensory details, so 'look' hard!)

· *Why?* Why is the character hiding or thinking about hiding? Motivation, after all, drives our characters.

It's now time for me to 'warm up'. Here goes…

> *This was no time to hide.*
> *True, the principal was stomping down the hallway, but how could we be sure she was looking for us?*
> *Okay, we had rigged the bowl of water to empty onto her head…and we had charged a pizza party to the school two weeks ago…and we did get on the intercom and ask for Mr. Flint to report to the office in the middle of math class, which gave Kelsey and Lindsay clear sailing to plant the Whoopee cushion…Come to think of it, I guess this was the perfect time to hide…*

So what will come of this story? Perhaps nothing. But I'm content that almost a hundred words flowed from my pen as I envisioned two kids huddled one afternoon in a school custodian's closet. And the piece is there to connect with some future writing project, if I so choose.

Plus, from this, I can:

· Delve into the kids' past.

· Change my characters from kids to adults (Heeeyyyy! I like that idea!).

· Project what happens in the next hour, day, week, or year.

· Start a dialogue between the two characters.

· Place them in a counselor's office or face-to-face with some rather irate parents.

If I were to revisit this prompt, an entirely different story might emerge. So, thanks to your own imagination, you're actually getting many more than 1000 prompts from this book. (Extremely generous of me, don't you think?)

How to use this book

1. Flip to any page in the book. Find a story idea that spurs your visualization process or begins to write itself and let it happen! (And for those whose mind's eye might need a little nudge, I've included a few intermittent graphics.)

2. Revisit prompts that didn't work a month ago. The preceding 672 hours may change your perception of those ideas.

3. Let my prompts serve only as springboards. Change their setting, character(s), character gender or motivation, tone of the spoken words. In other words, don't lock yourself into my idea.

4. Combine prompts to create interesting possibilities.

5. Create your own and write from your own prompts. Scrawl away in the margins for your own "can't miss" ideas.

Am I being too flexible and open-minded? Sorry, but that's the point of the book—to spark your own imagination and let you take over.

Have fun and fill those notebooks!

1. "All right!" snapped my sister. "It's time to separate the men from the boys!"

2. Just one nickel and I hit the jackpot!

3. I leaned toward the finish line…

4. "And the winner is…"

5. I knew I'd survive, but it wouldn't be pleasant…

6. The shiver went up my back…

7. This was no time for hysterics…

8. She would have to beat the train to the next town…

9. He closed his eyes and put out his hand…

10. "I'm not going to try it. YOU try it!"

11. The pumpkin-sized water balloon arched toward…

12. I looked around and couldn't figure out why everyone was cheering…

13. The sparkle in its eye told me… I would be safe/ I was in big trouble/others were on their way.

14. Every morning, it was the same routine…

15. Sure I wanted to see the world, but…

16. Safety/Freedom/Eternal wealth… was an inch away.

17. The neighbors' iguana was loose again. This was an opportunity I didn't expect…

18. "Stop right there!!"

19. The 'F' on my paper was the least of my worries…

20. I knew the answer, but I didn't dare say a word…

21. He woke up with only one thing on his mind…

22. Jupiter's atmosphere proved more challenging than I expected...

23. "Cover your eyes! Now!"

24. Her hair frizzed in every direction...

25. His ears pointed east and west...

26. He broke my heart, and now...

27. I didn't know what to do, so I bowed/curtsied/ate it...

28. What was a campfire story soon turned real...

29. My lip quivered, my hands shook...

30. "The secret to beautiful hair!" said the label...

31. She knew she had found the culprit. But now what?

32. "Niagara Falls? In a canoe?"

33. Playing hooky was not part of our plan...

34. "Let's play hooky," said our science teacher...

35. Who would have ever thought she would save the entire company?

36. "Where's your spirit of adventure?" asked my mom as... the speedometer hit 100/she checked her parachute/she loosened the lock on the lion's cage...

37. Title: Never to Return

38. Title: Moment of Glory

39. There was a reason the sign said, "DANGER"...

40. A single giggle started the insanity...

41. The balloon rose before I could...

42. "Welcome to our new school!" said the voice over the loud speaker...

43. "We don't think you belong here..."

44. 'Coward' was my middle name...

45. With each page I turned, I landed in a new...

46. "Get a grip, would ya?"

47. An uncontrollable urge consumed the doctor/ quarterback/mechanic/pastry chef/salesgirl/ hungry dog...

48. He had transformed into an action toy...

49. At that point, adrenalin took over...

50. "Here's your $20 million. Now go..."

51. All she needed was chocolate...

52. Gold fever gripped the community...

53. "Are you sure you can last?"

54. "So this is what the wild blue yonder really looks like..."

55. "Which way did he go?"

56. He stood before us. It was obvious this was no ordinary...

57. She actually complimented me!

58. I looked down. I really did have two left feet...

59. He was afraid to open the envelope…

60. This had to be the lamest conversation ever!

61. The pitbull whimpered and ran when Fifi showed up…

62. The waves carried me to freedom…

63. Geez, she was rude!

64. "So why do I have to throw the ball/spitwad/pie/party?"

65. He wasn't thrilled that people could see right through him…

66. My own mom didn't recognize me…

67. I had to find out what was in that room/box/notebook/trunk…

68. Yellow turned red and blue turned green…

69. "The guy's a hero!"

70. I wanted _____. Instead I got____.

71. "Don't take another step!"

72. I got the job. Now came the hard part...

73. I had to admit it. This time, Dad was right...

74. It looked *like* New York/my home/my room, but something was different...

75. "But, Mom! Yellow shoes?"

76. There, for all the world to see...

77. "Go right! No, left! No, straight!"

78. "What were you thinking?" asked my teacher/parents/friend/arch-enemy...

79. They were coming at me from all sides...

80. "What? Me afraid?

81. I passed a sign that said...

82. I needed a change...

83. "Why are you sitting at my desk?" asked his boss/the teacher/the police chief...

84. It dangled just inches from my fingertips...

85. I heard ticking...

86. "Are you ready?"

87. Crop circles everywhere...

88. The teacher looked at my paper...and then at me. "Well, well, well," she said...

89. The one-inch opening was all they needed...

90. Surprised? I was stupefied!

91. "Don't push your luck!"

92. Hanging on for dear life...

93. My hopes rose when I heard the car door slam...

94. "Don't leave angry! Just leave!"

95. The floor shifted to the right and then sank...

96. As I rounded the corner, I had the feeling my luck was about to change...

97. The moon glowed green, then orange...

98. The stairway to the heavens...

99. We had just sat down to eat...

100. It was time to meet my new family...

101. My first time alone behind the wheel...

102. As the prayer ended, his stomach gurgled "Ode to Joy"...

103. The ravenous/terrified/joyful St. Bernard jumped onto my lap...

104. A wall of snow blocked her last way out...

105. He had no idea how to swim, but he had no choice...

106. His first date with Anne and his mouth was numb from the novocaine...

107. If she created a distraction, she could...

108. This was no soap opera. This was my life...

109. He didn't want or deserve a birthday party, and yet...

110. She wasn't invited, but in she paraded with her two snootiest friends...

111. I first spotted it in my rearview mirror...

112. Charles raised his pencil and jabbed the air. "En garde!"

113. That was no snowball coming my way...

114. I reached into my closet. "Maybe this will help..."

115. "Sir, welcome to Las Vegas/Rome/Mt. Everest..."

116. "Eeeeww! Gross!" screamed the princess...

117. "I feel like I'm in a movie!"
     "You ARE in a movie!"

118. "That truck seems to be aiming for us..."

119. He dropped from the tree, directly into…

120. "It's the President on the phone!"

121. What began as a prank turned into…

122. As I crossed the finish line…

123. "No way will I trade with *her*!"

124. "Be there tonight," said the unknown voice, "with the money/fossils/tape/documents/ photographs…."

125. He switched the microwave setting to …

126. I didn't deserve this…

127. "Hey, kid! You forgot your…"

128. I was missing only one thing— my car/only friend/shoe/lucky charm/house/windshield/com- puter…

129. "Yeah, she did what I asked…and two things I told her not to…"

130. "Is it my imagination or did you just..."

131. The air was filled with...spitwads/smoke/confetti/hunks of food/burning embers...

132. This would be my home for the next year/week/six months/decade...

133. It was just a matter of time...

134. Somehow, the victory felt hollow...

135. "Are you sure you don't want just one?"

136. "Should there be flames coming out of that pan/the microwave/his nostrils/the tires?"

137. "You're on the air! Say something!"

138. We needed to move the game near the mud pit...

139. Falling, falling, falling...

140. Dangling above the stage was...

141. *I* had solved the burglaries. One problem: I was still the chief suspect...

142. 'Show and Tell' would never be the same...

143. "Well, he's no Prince Charming..."

144. There, at our front door, stood Elvis...

145. It was a birthday/Father's Day/Christmas/ Halloween I'd never forget...

146. Crashing through the ceiling...

147. "You are SO fired!"

148. Aaaah, music to my ears...

149. "Are you sure you want to order that?" asked the waitress...

150. There, tucked in her binder, were my lucky socks...

151. What the heck, no one was looking...

152. "Whatever you do, don't...open that door/look in the box/walk into the cave/eat that pie."

153. A simple smile set the wheels in motion...

154. He should NOT have planted that!

155. I could actually feel my brain waves...

156. The cloud followed him everywhere...

157. The mutant Slinky® crept down the steps...

158. I put on my magic glasses and sure enough...

159. The ball bounced off the ____ and...

160. "Do you call that dancing?"

161. "Mom! It happened again!"

162. Anti-gravity. That's what did it!

163. The little old lady/puppy/Girl Scouts/ballerinas didn't look all that dangerous...

164. "Okay," said the ____. "What we need is a plan..."

165. She opened the car's hood and found nothing. No engine, nothing...

166. It was Friday, so of course I had to...

167. With one push of a button...

168. "Free? Are you sure?"

169. The footprints looked familiar, but they led in a very unexpected direction...

170. There I was, about to be flattened by a giant bagel/marshmallow/pillow...

171. I didn't expect the curve in the road...

172. His pulse rate short-circuited the monitors...

173. The doctor chuckled/stroked his beard/ pushed a red button. "We've discovered the problem. You have..."

174. Everything I did, she did better...

175. It's as if I were looking in a mirror...

176. If he could just make it bounce...

177. "Activate all security forces!"

178. The TV show's theme song pounded in my head...

179. She slipped into the phone booth as a quiet, unassuming sales clerk and came out as ...

180. The only person left standing...

181. "How does he do that with his face/arms/legs/eyes/nose...?"

182. "Boss, the kid never ran out of energy!"

183. And so began the race for the last pizza/chair/wind-up toy..."

184. The hole in her pocket would prove costly...

185. His hopes were shattered...

186. The longer I stared, the more alive it became...

187. As I turned the doorknob, the laughter died/grew even louder...

188. The chicken had actually crossed the road!

189. "Really, Mr. Olsen, my dog DID eat my homework!"

190. The fashion police were coming to take me away...

191. Dreadful doesn't begin to describe it...

192. The cell phone rang for the fifth time...

193. "Hey Smith! Get that piano off your back!"

194. "Is that your final answer?"

195. The disbelieving minister looked at the bride/groom. "You don't?" he asked.

196. The ring in his nose reminded me...

197. Steam drifted upward from his ears/feet/fingertips...

198. It was going to be a lo-o-o-ooong day/night/morning/year/30 minutes...

199. The tree branches drooped whenever Maggie was sad...

200. I woke up nose-to-nose with a golden retriever/triceratops/fresh apple pie...

201. She/he was my last chance...

202. Hidden in the cereal box...

203. The closer I got to the painting, the more I smelled fresh-baked bread/salt air/roses...

204. It turned out to be a love/ransom/dismissal note...

205. He already owed the bank $20,000...

206. "Look!" She adjusted her stick pretzels. "I'm a walrus!"

207. His sad, brown eyes told me one thing...

208. Answering the ad proved to be a mistake...

209. "Yoga for kids? Sure I'll try it..."

210. "Pot roast/meat loaf/broccoli/braised eel...for dessert?"

211. The teacher began writing in hieroglyphics...

212. "Mom, I've got something to tell you…"

213. "Here he comes! Act like nothing's happened."

214. The worst advice I ever got…

215. It was like a reflex. Every time I…

216. This guy was a throwback to the 60's…

217. Her dog filled the back seat…

218. "So which one are you—Sleepy, Dopey, or Sneezy?"

219. "I'll see you in court!"

220. "Where's my dinner?" asked the cat.

221. "Well, back to square one…"

222. We couldn't back down now…

223. Her only ambition: to be obnoxious…

224. Everything he did turned out wrong…

225. "Who are you today—Dr. Jekyll or Mr. Hyde?"

226. "Ready? Now close your eyes and count back from twenty…"

227. They had everything and we had nothing…

228. We never expected our innocent little lemonade stand to…

229. It was pure joy/boredom/hate/love at first sight…

230. Title: Night of the Zombies

231. Title: Donald Trump Meets Forrest Gump

232. My cruel words hung in the air…

233. He had bit the hand that fed him…

234. Luckily, Superman does exist…

235. "Okay, soldiers/kids/Mr. President, pat your head and rub your stomach…"

236. The empty train eased into the terminal...

237. "Please turn your pockets inside out!"

238. "For the next hour, we will work on 'unlearn-ing'..."

239. He was never to return—in that form, that is...

240. The shirt revealed an important clue...

241. Moonbeams lit up the grimy dungeon...

242. The map was wrong. It had to be...

243. The poverty wasn't so bad. But the loneliness was...

244. "Sheesh! What amateurs! Don't they know..."

245. Perhaps the floor had been overwaxed just a bit...

246. "Yes, my name IS John Doe and this is my sis-ter Jane..."

247. So *that's* who owned the money/car/dog!

248. "No, I was *not* raised by wolves!"

249. The quarterback huddled everyone before the first play. Finally, she was in charge...

250. "Yes, I am a mild-mannered reporter and yes, I do know Lois Lane, but..."

251. The pounding on the door rattled the whole apartment...

252. "Leonardo, must you continue with all these weird inventions?"

253. The masked man approached 'The Mona Lisa' with his black felt pen...

254. Had that black cat broken the mirror under my ladder on purpose?

255. He flung his pocket protector across the room..."I am not a nerd!"

256. "What should I do with my life?"

257. I had no idea he was so popular...

258. He continued his never-ending trek up the down escalator...

259. It was the silliest argument I'd ever heard...

260. We had to go our separate ways...

261. I just wanted to fit in...

262. If only I were 15...

263. Another case solved. Or so we thought...

264. I never envisioned myself as a rock star...

265. "Throw me a rope!"

266. "Don't listen to them," said my sister...

267. The box kept vibrating...

268. The minute he bit into the tomato...

269. "Why should I trust you?"

270. The fastball came straight at my knees...

271. Three phones rang at once...

272. Our winning streak was in jeopardy...

273. The moon winked at me as I flew by...

274. Day-by-day, the 80-foot pine tilted closer to our house.

275. "So, which planet do you want to take over?"

276. Every time I itched, he scratched...

277. There was no turning back...

278. My foot was dead asleep and it was my turn to cross the stage...

279. I think I caught something...

280. I knew I shouldn't have picked up the phone...

281. With each new costume came a change of personality...

282. The homeless man held out his last quarter. "Here," he said, "you need it more than I do."

283. There was only one way to get her to stop eating/talking/running/twiddling her thumbs...

284. Daydreaming was my only solution...

285. "Don't be such a crybaby!"

286. I had finally found my mother/family/father/ home/wallet/other shoe...

287. The waves towered over my boat...

288. "I don't remember inviting you," she said with a sneer...

289. The eyes followed me all the way to...

290. The piggy bank was supposed to be empty...

291. There stood my coach/piano teacher/baby-sitter, hands on hips...

292. "A ten-year-old should be more responsible," she said to me.

293. He had the crazed eyes and rumpled wardrobe of a mad scientist...

294. We didn't expect the campground to be...

295. "Save the whales? What about me?"

ISBN 0-8383-1371

296. As thousands held their breath, the... fly ball came straight toward my mitt/football dropped to the ground/goalie reached with her gloved hand...

297. The door shut and he/she/it/they were gone...

298. "Which side of the road do people drive on?" my dad asked as he changed lanes...

299. "Stop, look, and listen!" We rolled our eyes...

300. He glided from one rooftop to the next...

301. The dandelion sticking out of her ear...

302. "I would help you, but my foot..."

303. He had a dozen good reasons to say 'no', but...

304. When the eagle/butterfly/elephant landed on my shoulder...

305. "I think," said the pilot, "that sandwich is headed straight for us..."

306. I never imagined my quirks would drive my boss nuts...

307. "Time to fix the ___. Just hand me that hammer..."

308. I had gained/lost 20 pounds in one day...

309. The furry team mascot went berserk...

310. Should I lie or should I risk my friendship?

311. "Very impressive," said my teacher. "Three straight 'F's."

312. The brickwork spelled out a very clear message...

313. "You weren't supposed to bring it back!"

314. I was his biggest fan and there I stood, holding his wallet...

315. She had shot off her mouth once too often...

316. Five minutes till 'Open House' and the classroom...

317. "You won't regret it," he said.

318. "Aha!"

319. I was tired of talking. I wanted action!

320. The river kept rising…

321. He cried 'wolf,' and sure enough…

322. I had absolutely wimped out!

323. "Go ahead! Dare to be different!"

324. I reached for Mom's hand and instead got a furry paw…

325. I looked for Washington's face on the dollar bill and saw my picture instead…

326. I couldn't help but look…

327. This might tickle a little bit…

328. "Why doesn't anyone believe me?"

329. I pulled back his sleeve and, instead of flesh, saw circuits and wires…

330. His coffee order lasted a full minute…

331. "What are you trying to sell me now?"

332. Joy…relief…confusion—I felt all three…

333. "Tell me this—why should I care?"

334. "Believe me, you were our last choice…"

335. "You're no fairy godmother!"

336. This guy really knew how to stand out in a crowd…

337. Once again, I lost the bet and it was now time to pay up…

338. I was 12, but I felt like 60…

339. The wrinkles in her clothing AND on her face disappeared within seconds…

340. Tattered bathrobe. Hair in curlers. She was enough to scare the kids AND their parents…

341. Could this frog really be the princess?

342. I realized I had a second chance…

343. "Close your eyes and open your hand…"

344. "I've got happy feet!"

345. The guy was a total Einstein…

346. Maybe, just maybe…

347. All the people I loved…

348. I tripped over a pollen grain…

349. I couldn't believe it! I was actually right!

350. He rose above us. "Let me teach you about levitation," he said.

351. This was more than a feud…

352. The date was June 55th…

353. The whole state of Illinois drifted past Ohio and on toward Pennsylvania…

354. "He called me a chucklehead!"

355. My gentle sneeze set off an ugly chain-reaction…

356. "Don't be such a 'Nervous Nellie!"

357. My foot tapped, my head bobbed…the disco music was working its magic…

358. Leaves sprouted from the walls…

359. This was my best practical joke ever…

360. He was a total pushover…

361. "You're making me a nervous wreck!"

362. I had never been an outcast before…

363. Finally! Free as a bird!

364. The revolution was on!

365. I rolled out my new vehicle and turned the key…

366. The alien landed in my cereal…

367. Our field trip started normally enough…

368. "What can I say? It was an impulse!"

369. "Well, it's over, it's definitely over..."

370. She plopped down right on the hot radiator...

371. Why *I* was cloned I'll never know...

372. "Hey, you! Outta that tree!"

373. "Just calm down," said the stranger, "and tell me what happened."

374. She was the only person who knew why I was balancing on top of the Ferris wheel...

375. "Dunklebottom, you have 24 hours to fix this little problem..."

376. Of all our little misadventures, this one would be the most challenging...

377. My butler bowed. "Whatever you wish, sir..."

378. "Quiet, please," she said to me, "and put on your bib..."

379. The rubber chicken kept appearing at the weirdest times...

380. The police chief showed up wearing a bulbous red nose and floppy shoes...

381. "I asked you not to..."

382. He just *had* to step on that banana peel...

383. "Are those really your ears?"

384. Somewhere in that Dumpster lay my ring/retainer/glasses/money/homework...

385. "And now," bellowed the announcer, "he-e-e-er-r-re's..."

386. Smack! Right on his...

387. "Yes," she said, "that's quite an impressive pie/head of hair/storm cloud/bicycle..."

388. It was the perfect time for the necktie/berry pie/can of tuna/couch to explode...

389. The stink bomb worked to perfection...

390. Just as I thought, her face DID freeze in that position!

391. She looked down from the high wire. The audience looked so-o-o-o small...

392. Healed! I was healed!

393. He looked around at the chimps, hippos, and elephants... "Do we really have to get married here?"

394. I swung open the refrigerator door...

395. "Good morning," said the voice. "Could I interest you in..."

396. They emptied the bucket down my shirt...

397. Riding the giraffe down Main Street attracted more than a few stares...

398. The theme park was mine, all mine...

399. He towered over me. "Nice to meet you," he squeaked...

400. "Tonight you will join us on your first snipe hunt..."

401. I couldn't figure out what they were gawking at...

402. "Awwww, can't Mr. Bully-Boy take a joke?"

403. What I held in my hands brought back fond/painful/hilarious memories...

404. No one's courage matched hers...

405. "Did you hear the one about..."

406. I took the baboon by hand and walked into the vet's office/furniture store/china shop/restaurant/church...

407. My cheek spasms worsened...

408. A football game on TV, a bowl of popcorn, and all alone...

409. "What could possibly go wrong?" asked my soon-to-be former friend...

410. "Waiter! There's a _____ in my _____!"

411. It couldn't have happened to a better showoff...

412. We would never make it to the airport on time...

413. "I don't know about you, but I'm outta here!"

414. What did the kids/dog/visitors/trees/cops know that I didn't?

415. All he needed was a little practice...

416. "Today, class, is 'Break the Rules Day'..."

417. "Conquer your fears!" said the wizard and he disappeared...

418. My dreams were shattered...

419. "Not a good move," said the chemistry teacher as she wiped...

420. "Quick! Out that window!"

421. These weren't my parents/shoes/teeth/usual excuses...

422. I had to break that window!

423. Within an hour, she would have three new sisters...

424. One look at me and Dracula turned and bolted for the door...

425. I now had two mysteries to solve...

426. Her deafening snores interrupted the board meeting...

427. Once again, he was the last one chosen...

428. "I'd like you to meet my invisible friend..."

429. He was all of four feet tall, yet no one dared disobey...

430. There was an old woman who lived in a...

431. "Me? An astronaut?"

432. The witch shook her head. "Your spots should be gone by now…"

433. Sure enough—there stood the FedEx guy with a caged …

434. *This* tooth fairy wore dentures…

435. Would the rains ever stop?

436. "You should start a new club!"

437. This was the third straight night it had eaten my homework…

438. The chocolate smudge was my first clue…

439. The baby grabbed my nose and wouldn't let go…

440. I thought I would be babysitting a human…

441. She smacked me with her book/clipboard/sandwich…

442. I finally figured out my mistake. But was it too late?

443. Just when they thought they knew everything...

444. My surprise for Mom and Dad...

445. Driving without a windshield...

446. This was one spoiled kid...

447. There was only one other thing they could play
catch with...

448. The wishbone snapped and my life was never
the same...

449. Same board game, but this time the money was
real...

450. Even as I rang the doorbell, I knew...

451. "Mom, why is Dad running through sprin-
klers?"

452. She had no choice—she had to join the circus...

453. I put up my feet on the principal's desk, folded
my hands behind my head, and ...

454. "This is going to hurt me more than it'll hurt you," he said. I doubted that.

455. "Time for pasta!" my friend said as he whisked away the silverware...

456. I flicked the switch. "Testing, testing," I said into the school's microphone...

457. The floor creaked under me, but I hadn't moved a muscle...

458. The front door closed behind me, but the lion never stirred...

459. Mom had said we could stay up late, but she forgot that...

460. The little girl screamed that I had taken her purse...

461. "So is it true that a tongue can stick to a frozen pole?"

462. "Hey, guys, can I go with you?" We cringed...

463. I tried to see the word in my mind. What WAS the next letter?

464. "This is no time to cry/laugh/clean your room...!"

465. I could give the money back or...

466. As her tears touched the floor, they turned to gold...

467. Clad in flowing white robes, the winged creature...

468. The desperate cowboy threw the saddle on my back and yelled, "Giddyap!"...

469. Fido jumped up on the table. "Sit!" he said. I sat.

470. "All you ever do is fly by the seat of your pants!" said my teacher...

471. Little did they know...

472. I reached back with the bowling ball, took aim, and followed through. One problem...my fingers were stuck.

473. Her prize roses had shrunk six inches since yesterday…

474. "Clearly," said my dad, "you've been overprotected."

475. "Go to your room!" Mom said to Dad.

476. "Shake hands!" said the werewolf.

477. He gave a head fake and ran for the door…

478. My family…whacked-out, but they were all I had…

479. The Whoopee Cushion® was in place…

480. My boat sped toward the jagged reef…

481. Grounded for a month…

482. "My gawd! What a sourpuss!"

483. "Follow the yellow brick what?"

484. "Quit watching me!" yelled the mime…

485. The alarm sounded. We looked at each other…

486. He DID have eyes in the back of his head...

487. She needed a favor and she needed it now...

488. "Your fingerprints are all over the cookie jar!"

489. I put in the videotape and pressed 'play'...

490. "Act your age!" she said. I giggled and put the pacifier back in my mouth...

491. "Yes, kids, today the theater is yours!"

492. Her fake nose and glasses actually fooled the security guards...

493. "Excuse me, sir, but would you be interested in a trip around the world?"

494. "All right, kids! As soon as you're done with lunch, it'll be time for bed..."

495. The new student's suit of armor creaked as she entered...

496. I hid in the only possible place...

497. Dad's voice rang through the house. "Are you done with your homework/vegetables/nose job?"

498. Who would've thought one rubber band could cause so much trouble?

499. "Son/young lady/Rover..., you need to get a job."

500. "Someone should put a bell on him," she said...

501. My grandma called me 'gifted'. So did my teacher...

502. "Someday you'll thank me."
I rolled my eyes.

503. It was time to change my name...

504. "Boy," said my teacher, "if only I were 15..."

505. I didn't appreciate his cracking a raw egg over my head…

506. Sure I was lazy, but it usually paid off…

507. I had never had a chauffeur before…

508. There, on the JumboTron®, for all the world to see…

509. As long as Mom wasn't looking, the dog slept wherever he wanted…

510. My friends had deserted me…

511. "I have a date and I need the bathroom!"

512. The principal leaned back in her chair…a little too far.

513. I had to learn to talk all over again…

514. "Let me tell you a thing or two about your dad," said Grandma.

515. "Hey! Who invited the kangaroos/monkeys/dogs to the reception?"

516. As he sprinted for the TV room, his pajama sleeve caught the doorknob...

517. I couldn't decide which friend to help...

518. "Any questions?"
One hand rose from the back of the room...

519. "If you turn that page," said a voice from the book, "you'll be sorry..."

520. "All right, which one of you drives a white Model T?"

521. The ice cube was warm to the touch...

522. All I wanted was sleep/freedom/a million dollars/one loyal friend/a dog...

523. "Trick or treat? In the middle of June?"

524. Someone had blabbed...

525. She rolled the quarter toward me...

526. He banged on the rock twice...

527. She chuckled, twirled the ring on her fingers, and the skies opened up...

528. I wasn't used to running with six legs…

529. "When in doubt," announced my friend, "go shopping."

530. "Go ahead and make a wish," said the diabolical librarian/dentist/nurse/store owner/waitress…

531. "Kids," said my dad at dinner, "it's time to move…"

532. I was starting to grate on her nerves, and I was loving it…

533. I opened my mouth to speak.
"Don't butt in!" she snapped.

534. A drop of sweat trickled down to the tip of my nose…

535. This had to be some kind of record…

536. "1-2-3-pull!"

537. The rumors were true after all…

538. The principal wandered in wearing pink leotards…

539. My knees locked up, as the bull rushed towards me...

540. But I didn't want to be a secret agent/teacher/baby again/frog/brain surgeon...

541. She said we should get close to nature, but this was ridiculous...

542. "You have to defend yourself!" said Mary Louise...

543. All he wanted was to feel needed...

544. "Don't say you're sorry. Just fix it!"

545. She knew she'd never be back...

546. "Whoa! Stereo-parents!"

547. "Mr. _____, you have been found guilty of..."

548. This was going to be an interesting parent conference...

549. "At the top of the hour," said the voice, "you'll be changing species..."

550. As I spoke, my words floated through the air and …

551. "Okay, kids, grab a balloon and we'll begin our journey…"

552. "Yes, I'm psychic. So what?"

553. "Rapunzel! It's time for that haircut!"

554. I would follow the baboon as long as it would let me…

555. This was no game…

556. I saw it in the store window and couldn't stop thinking about it…

557. He wished for the wrong thing and now…

558. "Just sit down here and I'll teach you to cook…"

559. "Could you please move your dinosaur?"

560. Face first into the bowl of ice cream…

561. Abracadabra!

562. The mild rattling of the windows seemed innocent enough…

563. "Time for you to move to another seat!" snapped the usher…

564. Without warning, my friends crawled under their desks…

565. The kids stood at attention, and then, one by one…

566. The camera followed us everywhere…

567. His imagination kicked into overdrive…

568. This was no time to sleep/relax/laugh/cower/ watch TV…

569. Alone, in the corner of the playground…

570. "So, did you forget how to…"

571. It didn't matter what he said, I still…

572. The top of the jar unscrewed itself...

573. All those years of friendship...

574. The zebras/chimps/kangaroos/parakeets finally took over...

575. The class/parents/team/leaders erupted in laughter...

576. When the two walked into the room, I knew there'd be trouble...

577. Thirty pairs of eyes staring right through me...

578. As I flew through the air, I concluded she was stronger than I thought...

579. And with the words, "I'm ba-a-ack!", our lives went topsy-turvy...

580. "First the asteroid belt, then the Big Dipper! Where next?"

581. "I repeat, you...are invisible/have won/have lost/have no hair!"

582. "Hey! This hypnosis thing works pretty well!"

583. She flicked on the flashlight and peered into the closet...

584. I didn't mean to be funny, but...

585. He claimed it was lasagna...

586. "Rock 'n roll just might be the answer..."

587. I/They/The feather/The car...wouldn't budge...

588. The only way to put the car in reverse was to push with my left leg...

589. His eye was bigger than my whole head...

590. Forty floors was a long way...

591. "Not yet!!"

592. "There! Good as new!"

593. "What happens if I pull this?"

594. "Please! Just leave me alone!"

595. "How are your reflexes?" asked the pastry chef.

596. My shoulders tightened as I turned the knob/ started the engine/reached to my back pocket/ shook her hand/thought of an excuse...

597. Caught in the act!

598. The anti-gravity vest worked wonders...

599. The motion-activated robot soon developed its own instincts...

600. One loose thread would prove to be his downfall...

601. "Don't clap! Just throw money!"

602. Let's just say our new neighbors had some odd customs...

603. "No need to worry. Things are going to get easier..."

604. "We're just going to have to learn, and fast!"

605. "Mr. Smith, your comment was rude and ill-timed..."

606. If this didn't work out, well,...

607. "Hey! Use a baseball bat, not a rolling pin!"

608. "Excuse me, your shoe is ringing..."

609. "Young man, you'll need to pay your dinner bill before leaving..."

610. Title: Dancing Pants

611. The shivering wouldn't stop...

612. I wasn't sure which of his three hands I should shake...

613. Tumbling down a ravine was not my idea of vacation...

614. I stood up straight and waited to face her big brother...

615. Trampled by the ravenous rabbit...

616. "So what does your invention do?"

617. It was an adrenaline rush I never expected...

618. He spread his arms and the winds lifted him away...

619. "Time to switch faces!"

620. I opened my lunch and out scurried...

621. The two trees greeted each other with a gentle shake of their branches...

622. I tucked the steaming pizza under my arm and... raced for the goal line/bolted for the door/sidled into the crowd/ran for the church/skipped to class...

623. Every one of my thoughts was instantly broadcast to my classmates...

624. "Of course, I did the Hokey-Pokey! Isn't that what's it's all about?"

625. "Do as I say, not as I do!"

626. And, with one heroic leap, she…

627. "So," said the principal/her parents/the spy, "tell us about yourself."

628. "Take my pulse!"

629. And I saw her standing there…

630. "Help! I need somebody!"

631. I broke out into a medley of Elvis songs…

632. Fifteen people hanging onto one parachute…

633. "Please peel this off my meal!"

634. The rainbow sunrise greeted the travelers…

635. This little piggy…

636. What big teeth you have!

637. I'll huff and I'll puff and…

638. This was no gentle giant…

639. "Step aside. I'll catch it…"

640. The bike's wheels rattled, then loosened...

641. "I've never seen someone flex their ears like that..."

642. 555-4263...I should have known.

643. April Fools!

644. My science project surprised everyone, especially me.

645. "And you're not feeling guilty?"

646. "Friends forever?" I asked. She paused...

647. Aaaah, my favorite time of day...

648. Boy, did I owe him!

649. The music seeped out of every crack in the wall...

650. Boom-shakka-lakka...

651. "I'm afraid you're going to have to leave."

652. All I had to do was make sure she was safe...

653. He smelled like a walking fruit salad...

654. My mother glared at us and signaled for a time out...

655. The magic amulet/arm band/pinky ring/wig/ car key... was working to perfection...

656. "But I ordered pie!"

657. "Isn't this Disneyland?"

658. He wasn't exactly thrilled to be there...

659. The steps led up, then down, then...

660. "Who me?"

661. "I'm not old, I'm experienced..."

662. "Welcome to Shnookeropolis" said the sign.

663. If he left now, he could dodge the dreaded question...

664. The sundae/stuffed giraffe/bedpost/book reached to the ceiling...

665. The deal was off...

666. The puck/ball was in the net. And so was I...

667. This lady did NOT need a megaphone...

668. "Please don't marry me!"

669. They called him 'Chunk'.

670. "I'm not sure your country even exists..."

671. The plane was airborne, but I wasn't...

672. "It's not me, it's you!"

673. "It's not you, it's me!"

674. I hated when he called me that...

675. Locked in a room with a book, a wrench, and a rubber band...

676. The sun slipped over the hills...

677. "I'll have it to you by tomorrow."

678. "Are you sure that's me?"

679. As I unwrapped the Snickers bar/strolled through the vacant lot/warmed up the engine, an idea popped into my head...

680. Once again, the sun shined as rain pelted the roof...

681. I was out of paper and ink, but I had to write this story...

682. The castle shook with every clap of thunder...

683. "Now give me one good reason why I should..."

684. I faked right, then left, and...

685. This was no foreign country. This was another planet...

686. Just ten easy payments!

687. Her eyes drifted to another place, another time...

688. "I think I've met your brother/mother/father/ Weird Uncle Al..."

689. The faster I pedaled, the slower I went...

690. His piercings formed a perfect star...

691. Luckily, I had remembered nothing...

692. "Say what?"

693. Everyone was at my surprise party, but me...

694. "It's the mayor of Gooberopolis on line one..."

695. I could've sworn it was Saturday...

696. Up around the bend my future awaited...

697. "Family and friends, we are gathered here to-day..."

698. "We were going to test drive the car, not steal it!"

699. "You are one in a million," he said to us.

700. I couldn't control myself...

701. "Stop the countdown!"

702. It was time to go underground...

703. The glow in the distance should have been a warning to all of us...

704. Pizza! I must have pizza!

705. I noticed he had grown another horn...

706. "I may be mistaken, but I think your hair is on fire..."

707. "Your bill is two million dollars. Will that be cash or check?"

708. She knew exactly what her friend was thinking...

709. He put two coins into the machine and waited...

710. The design on his shirt transformed every 30 seconds...

711. His toes ached, his fingernails ached, his hair ached...

712. My city had disappeared...

713. "You are funky beyond words!"

714. I could've sworn I told you...

715. So confident, so cool, and yet...

716. The cupcake oozed out of my pocket...

717. Go ahead, make me an offer...

718. The cream pie fit his hand perfectly...

719. He pushed and pulled and shoved, but still...

720. With the flick of her wand,...

721. I tried to blend in with the crowd...

722. "What do you think of my pet iguana/elephant/cobra/paramecium?"

723. "I always keep my gum here..."

724. "Could you please point me to the castle?"

725. He tried to look interested, but he kept nodding off...

726. We needed a new recipe and we needed it now...

727. No matter how hard I tried...

728. I had to get to the bank and all I had was this stupid unicycle...

729. "Ohhh, THAT elephant!"

730. "Pass the peas now!"
And boy, did I...

731. He didn't just walk. He strutted...

732. Face-to-face with a velociraptor...

733. We raised our trumpets to our lips and aimed...

734. "I hate to bother you, Captain, but I think we lost a propeller..."

735. They were sure the island was deserted...

736. Yes, I needed a disguise, but this?

737. He fit in the palm of her hand...

738. All this time, the townspeople had thought he couldn't walk/hear/talk/see...

739. And in the darkness, another pair of eyes popped open...

740. "Okay, you have five minutes..."

741. It all started with a can of unwanted red paint...

742. We were all in slow motion...

743. A brown suit, tie-dyed socks, and lemon yellow running shoes...

744. Just one little taste wouldn't hurt...

745. No matter how hard she scrubbed...

746. The archaeologist emerged from the cave...

747. "You look oddly familiar..."

748. I scribbled furiously and passed her the note...

749. She took her ball and went home, and there we stood...

750. "Hello, Juliet. My name is Skunkwort and this is my wretched little brother Romeo..."

751. This time, the race went to the smartest...

752. Psst, buddy, hand me that...

753. I glanced at the TV. Whoa! What was *I* doing on the news?

754. The light bulb melted in my hands...

755. "Sir, do you know why I pulled your car over?"

756. I sat back while the furniture rearranged itself...

757. The dusty old trunk I didn't mind. But I did mind the hairy hand crawling out of it...

758. "One hundred dollars for a piece of bubble gum?"

759. "Someone left the lighthouse unguarded!"

760. The principal folded her arms and said, "Okay, Mr. Smartypants, the school is yours for the day..."

761. The dentist beamed at me as he revved up his mega-drill...

762. "It's obvious to me," said my doctor, "that you need to eat as many sweets as possible..."

763. The dog blinked his eyes and flapped his ears...

764. POOF! It had worked just as planned...

765. The car swerved, spun, and sprung skyward...

766. A hand popped out of the dishwasher and a voice said, "There's still room for two more plates..."

767. And with the snap of my fingers...

768. "Mom! We have a visitor!"

769. So I wasn't alone after all...

770. As I wrote my answer on the board,...

771. The glint of her eye told me she oozed magic...

772. Oh sure, the potato looked like my teacher, but who would have thought...

773. I reached into the cabinet and, without looking, grabbed...

774. Fatigue was dragging me down, but curiosity pulled me along...

775. Mrs. Ripsnort glared at Frederick...

776. Unlike every other tree in the orchard, this one never lost a leaf or changed colors. And it always...

777. I blinked and it appeared. I blinked again and it was gone...

778. "Mr. _____, could you please report to the principal's office?"

779. Yes, sir, I do believe that is Bigfoot...

780. But I didn't want to be a hero...

781. "You want me to what?"

782. The walls were actually closing in on me...

783. I reached for my wallet.
"No need," said the waitress. "See that lady over there?"

784. The minute my white paint touched the wall...

785. I sat back and watched the hysteria...

786. The hooded man checked his watch and paced outside my front door...

787. "I think I'm going to need that steering wheel..."

788. The snow drifted silently down to the desert oasis...

789. As he reached for the drumstick, it stood up and hopped away...

790. Shelves of toys, games, and candy tumbled behind me...

791. A hundred miles back, the sign said,
     "Holdenville 50 miles." Still no
     Holdenville…

792. "Of course, it's me. Who else would you ex-
     pect?"

793. I looked at my empty plate. I'm pretty sure I
     had ordered more than this…

794. Every ten minutes, the dinner table turned 90
     degrees to the right…

795. When its wings began flapping like a chicken's,
     I was pretty sure this was no ordinary air-
     plane…

796. The maple leaf fell to the forest floor. Such an
     insignificant event. Or was it?

797. "It's time to storm the kitchen!" commanded

798. One look at that baby told me…

799. The pictures on the wall vibrated and the flood-
     lights pulsated red and blue…

800. "Transmogrify now!" ordered the magician.

801. But why was *I* in the cage?

802. "Well, I hope you learned your lesson!"

803. "I didn't mean what I said!"

804. "I meant exactly what I said!"

805. "Look kid, I'm busy, so take off!"

806. "Face your friends and admit it!"

807. The only way he could get to Hawaii was by taxi...

808. The fortune teller fidgeted then looked at me and said,...

809. When the dog twitched, I twitched...

810. The planets lined up and drifted together to another galaxy...

811. I could have sworn that couch was blue when I was here last...

812. My toes were warmed up. "Okay," I said, "Where's the piano?"

813. A solitary figure emerged from the fog-shrouded beach...

814. "If I jump high enough, maybe, just maybe..."

815. She was down to her last possession...

816. I was a muddy mess, but I rang the doorbell anyway...

817. They were sending me to Las Vegas...

818. A birthday gift wrapped in aluminum foil. It had to be...

819. He refused! He actually refused!

820. Stars...everywhere he looked.

821. Title: Lessons From My Brother (Sister, Mother, Father...)

822. Title: Precious As Gold

823. "This is the Super Bowl and you want *me* to call the plays?"

824. Title: A Flurry of Fur

825. Colors danced as the piano played...

826. Done! I was finally done...

827. Tears would not help this time...

828. The stack of money towered over me...

829. I could not afford to get sidetracked...

830. There had to be an easier way out of this maze...

831. "Let me at that cat!" growled the mouse...

832. "Now that's something I've never seen," said the cop/mountain climber/quarterback/ fashion designer/ carpenter...

833. The driving snow turned to cotton candy...

834. The dog's gentle snores marked my last peaceful moment for the next two weeks…

835. The rain cloud followed me down the block…

836. The license plate said it all…

837. I had never been in a hot-dog eating contest before…

838. All I wanted was a loaf of bread and a quart of milk. Instead, I…

839. The microwave had a mind of its own…

840. "Of course you can trust me…"

841. "I don't want it!"
"Well, don't leave it with me."

842. "Stop grumbling and pick out a dress!"

843. The envelope opened itself...

844. The detective, all of 12 years old, scratched his fake beard and...

845. Sand castles as far as the eye could see...

846. The first day of school, and THIS had to happen...

847. "This job was supposed to be simple, but noooo-o-o. You just..."

848. I was out of wishes...

849. Bad enough that he was an archenemy, but now he...

850. I zigged when I should have zagged...

851. Ten yards from the goal line...

852. "What's this?" she asked...

853. "Your history knowledge is impressive," said the teacher. "But this is math class..."

854. "Well, what do you think?" asked the painter/inventor/sculptor…

855. His 'to-do' list was up to 99 items…

856. "Just snap your fingers and…"

857. That tree was just begging to be climbed…

858. What a collection of miscreants!

859. The wind shifted with every wag of his tail…

860. The trap door revealed…

861. For the third straight day, she was waiting for me…

862. A tasty concoction it wasn't, but it definitely did what he promised…

863. She was running! She was actually running!

864. A bluish aura surrounded her as she stood at the mountaintop…

865. A heptagonal sandwich. My mom was getting weirder by the day…

866. 'Twas the day after Christmas and all through the house...

867. I leaned over to greet our little guest...

868. "I can't think what to write next!" cried the author.
"Let me help," said a soft voice...

869. "I think I found your problem," said the repair-man.

870. *Something* made the candles flicker...

871. "Do you know it's against the law to drive backwards on a one-way street?"

872. "Hey! You with the bolts in your head!"

873. "Jeez, George, you certainly look hairy to-day..."

874. From my window, I could see the Eiffel Tower...

875. Scaling the Empire State Building was not ex-actly...

876. The shark approached…

877. I was sure the golf ball/balloon/meteorite landed there…

878. The light turned green and everybody…

879. This time when the teacher rang the bell…

880. No matter what words I typed, other words appeared…

881. Title: Alone in the Theater

882. Title: The Magic Chair

883. Before my eyes, my friend had slipped away to another dimension…

884. Finishing my homework was now the least of my worries…

885. "Mom! The FBI's here to see you!"

886. The dog grinned and shook my hand. "It's a deal!" he said…

887. "I'm not so sure it's alive..."

888. "Fifty pushups!" ordered the irate nun/grand-mother/chef...

889. Why would they think I wanted to be a doctor/clown/news reporter?

890. Waves crashed through the kitchen...

891. Pots and pans clanged out a familiar tune...

892. "I've never flown in a space shuttle before..."

893. My newest hairdo surprised even me...

894. Title: The Ultimate Dilemma

895. "Oh, great. *Now* you tell me!"

896. "Sure. And my name's Peter Rabbit..."

897. A banana split for breakfast. I knew right then...

898. Every aisle in the store, filled with...

899. The little twerp had snitched on me...

900. "A halo? Above *his* head?"

901. The handwriting sample matched the signature...

902. Cacophonous! That's the best word to describe it...

903. Five people at a time, vanishing...

904. Riding the rapids with my bike...

905. "Hey, Pretty Boy! Nice car!"

906. "What makes you think this will change his mind?"

907. He handed out the tests and immediately my mind went blank...

908. Just blend this peanut butter with this mashed broccoli...

909. He hoped burying it would solve his problems...

910. The mice danced across the bridge of his nose...

911. Nothing could hide that rotten egg smell...

912. "Just hide behind me!"

913. "Why didn't you tell me you've been working three jobs?"

914. That was no rabbit Mr. Snarkle pulled out of his hat...

915. "Since when do you have to know everything about me?"

916. As we approached the stranger, I knew...

917. The ten bucks in my shoe would come in handy...

918. No one could play the air guitar like she could...

919. "I cannot tell a lie, I..."

920. She blamed it all on me...

921. When he strolled inside still wearing sunglasses, I should have known...

922. "Let's just squirrel this away for another day..."

923. The sign said, STOP YUPPIES!/WE'RE BEING WATCHED!/LONG LIVE ALIENS/WATCH FOR FALLING DONUTS...

924. She could no longer hide her feelings...

925. I knew who did it, but I wouldn't dare tell...

926. Four dogs and five cats?

927. Somehow, I had to fool my boss...

928. Why did I have to eat *this*?

929. The muzzle wasn't working...

930. "Okay, here's the plan. At 2:00, when he's out of the room, we'll..."

931. "I'll tell you the secret, but first..."

932. Was it really worth it to walk all that way to school? I stopped and considered my choices...

933. All five of us leaned over to listen...

934. "You deal the cards and I'll distract the teacher..."

935. The elevator music was driving me crazy...

936. I had to keep a straight face for the next 30 seconds...

937. These people were willing to believe anyone's gossip...

938. Somewhere between the cafeteria and the playground, the vice-principal had lost a whole classroom of kids...

939. Goosebumps as big as BB's...

940. Crowds poured into the street...

941. The dust cloud barreled toward us...

942. The backpack was our only hope...

943. This battle of wits would not last long...

944. "Here, hook this bungee cord to your belt..."

945. My first night of backyard camping and who should show up but...

946. This time, celebrities wanted *my* autograph...

947. The ice cream truck/police/flowers arrived just in time...

948. "Awww, she's just showing off..."

949. He shook her hand and received a jolt of electricity...

950. "Hey, you! We need a stunt man!"

951. Our pleasure cruise turned into a police chase...

952. His quest took a detour...

953. Finally, a demolition derby for teachers/kids/teachers and kids...

954. This was one water sport we'd never seen...

955. Finally! Vacation!

956. "All right, all you rapscallions! Line up to the right!"

957. "Don't kick *me*! Kick the ball!"

958. It was the worst possible time to yell 'fire'...

959. After I lost the game, my teammates carried me off ...

960. Perhaps I blew out the candles a bit too hard...

961. I tossed my hat in the air and down came...

962. Just me, my rubber ducky, and a shark with a real bad attitude...

963. I was on a train to nowhere...

964. She opened my file and out popped...

965. As the crowd groaned, I grinned...

966. "What they don't know won't hurt them..."

967. "You're just plain nosey!"

968. At three in the morning, the library took on a whole new aura...

969. I was starting to like summer camp...

970. "This soda tastes funny…"

971. Finally! Someone else who wore his clothes inside out.

972. "Hey! I'm not your servant!"

973. The money kept spewing out of the automatic teller…

974. Where was she going to rent a camel?

975. "I'm no wizard!"

976. Finally, a reason to celebrate!

977. Suddenly, she was inspired…

978. This sounded like a get-rich-quick scheme…

979. "I don't need a bodyguard/my vegetables/a tuxedo/my friends…"

980. The safe had to be somewhere in this room…

981. His wall was covered with…

982. "Go ahead, have a taste…"

983. This had been a summer to remember...

984. How she became our boss was a mystery to us all...

985. "Step back, this is my specialty..."

986. The flame crept toward the box of fireworks...

987. The scooter had a mind of its own...

988. "I've never seen a sculpture made out of butter before..."

989. "MY parents as chaperones? No way!"

990. Fashion was her life...

991. They pelted him with pizza slices/tomatoes/globs of paint...

992. "Finish this project and I'll give you a day off..."

993. We could tell our soccer coach was desperate...

994. "Donuts for everyone!" screamed the sixth-graders...

995. When that food hit the plate, he knew...

996. At the time, hiding under the bed seemed like a good idea...

997. Let's just set this trap and we'll be on our way...

998. Her laboratory was the first of its kind...

999. He couldn't shake this recurring dream...

1000. I had been warned...

NOTES

NOTES